LIFE CYCLES

Potatoes

by Melanie Mitchell

Lerner Publications Company · Minneapolis

This is a **potato.**

There are many kinds of potatoes.

How do potatoes grow?

Potatoes grow from pieces
of other potatoes.

Potatoes have small **dents**
called eyes.

The eyes can grow new
potato plants.

A potato piece is planted.

Roots and a **stem** grow
from it.

The potato plant grows
bigger.

It makes flowers.

Where are the potatoes?

They are growing
underground.

The potato plant dies.

Now it is time to dig up the potatoes.

People will eat some of the
potatoes.

The rest will be saved to
grow new potato plants.

Life Cycle of a Potato

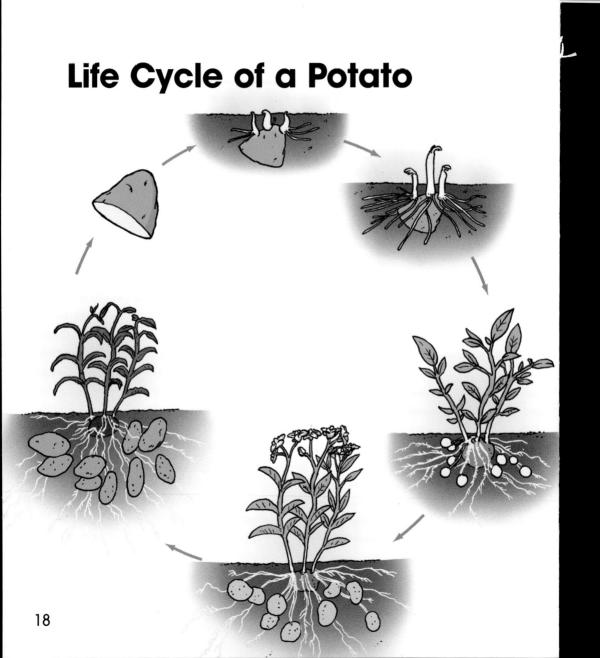

Potatoes

Potatoes are grown in many different places. They can grow in hot deserts and cold mountain areas. In the United States, potatoes are grown in every state.

Potatoes grow quickly. The life cycle of a potato lasts between 90 and 120 days. This means a potato piece can be planted and in 90 days it is time to dig up the new potatoes.

Potato Facts

 A potato is about 80 percent water.

 There are more than 5,000 kinds of potatoes.

 Idaho produces more potatoes than any other state in the United States.

 China produces more potatoes than any other country in the world.

A person who watches TV a lot and never exercises is called a couch potato.

 Thomas Jefferson first served french fries in the United States around 1802.

Instant potato flakes are sometimes used to look like snow in the movies.

Glossary

 dents – pushed-in parts on a surface

 potato – a kind of vegetable that grows underground

 roots – part of a plant that grows down into the ground

 stem – part of a plant that usually grows above the ground

 underground – below the earth's surface

Index

The photographs in this book are reproduced through the courtesy of: © Dwight Kuhn, front cover, pp. 7, 8, 9,11,13,15; Panos Pictures: © Sean Sprague, p.2; Agricultural Research Service, USDA, pp. 3, 12, 14,16, 17; © Todd Strand/Independent Pictures Service, pp. 4, 5, 6; © Karlene Schwartz, p. 10.

Illustration on page 18 by Tim Seeley.

Lerner Publications Company
A division of Lerner Publishing Group
241 First Avenue North
Minneapolis, MN 55401 U.S.A.

Website address: www.lernerbooks.com

Library of Congress Cataloging-in-Publication Data

Mitchell, Melanie S.
         Potatoes / by Melanie Mitchell.
            p.   cm. — (First step nonfiction) (Life cycles)
         Summary: A basic overview of the life cycle of a potato.
         ISBN: 0–8225–4612–4 (lib. bdg. : alk. paper)
         1. Potatoes—Life cycles—Juvenile literature. [1. Potatoes.]
      I. Title. II. Series.
      SB211.P8 M62 2003
      635'.21—dc21   2002004871

Manufactured in the United States of America
1 2 3 4 5 6 – AM – 08 07 06 05 04 03

12/03